*Montessori Manor* SCHOOL
P.O. Box 111
Phoenix, MD 21131
410/683-1771

# ANDY AND HIS DADDY

*a book for children and their parents*

by

## ALINE D. WOLF

With my thanks to Peggy Curran, Paula Benjamin, Ann Marie Swartz, Grace O'Connor, Mary Martone and Gerald Wolf for editorial assistance and to Charlie, Wendy, Steffie and Andy Wolf for sharing their family activities with our readers.

Photographs by Gerald P. Wolf, Charles J. Wolf, Wendy Wolf and Aline D. Wolf

Design by Jana Stanford-Sidler

ISBN #0-939195-14-3

Parent Child Press
PO Box 675, Hollidaysburg, PA 16648
(814) 696-7512

"If we were to establish a primary principle it would be to constantly allow the child's participation in our lives. For he cannot learn to act if he does not join in our actions, just as he cannot learn to speak if he does not hear . . .

"To extend to the child this hospitality, to allow him to participate in our work, can be difficult, but it costs nothing. Our time is a far more precious gift than material objects."

Maria Montessori

This is Andy.

He is two years old.

H|e lives with
his mommy,

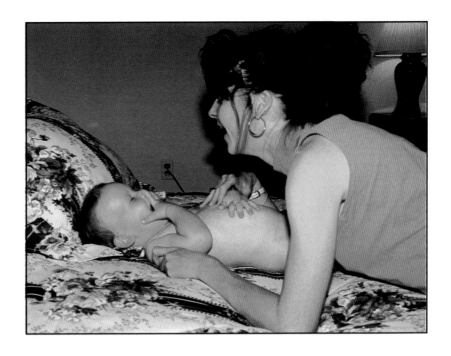

his daddy,

his big sister, Steffie,

and Buffy, their Cocker

Spaniel dog.

On weekday mornings, Andy helps Daddy to get ready for the office. He watches Daddy polishing his shoe.

Then Andy polishes the other shoe.

# H
e holds the shoehorn for Daddy,

and he pulls Daddy's laces tight.

$T$hen Andy takes Daddy's things off the dresser,

and puts Daddy's pen in his shirt pocket.

$A$fter Daddy goes to the office, Andy tries to dress himself,

but Mommy has to help him with his pants.

Mommy lets Andy put the plates in the dishwasher.

Somedays she lets him wash the plates in the sink.

He helps Mommy to vacuum the carpet,

and then he goes outside to throw his red ball in the basket.

A ndy loves the weekends when Daddy doesn't have to go to his office. On Saturday morning he follows Daddy downstairs. See how he holds the low railing that Daddy built for him.

Andy and Daddy get the eggs ready for breakfast. Daddy tells Andy how to crack each eggshell gently.

Then Daddy opens the shells and puts the eggs in a bowl.

Andy beats the eggs with a fork.

Next he wipes the counter

and gets the frying pan out
of the cupboard.

Daddy and Andy watch
while Steffie scrambles the eggs.

D addy puts the toast in the toaster,

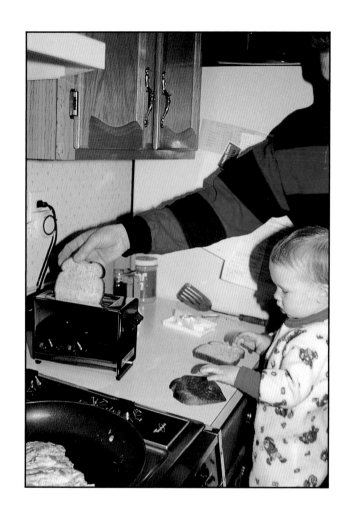

and Andy pushes it down.

T he toast is hot, so Andy blows on it.

T hen he butters his toast

and carries his plate over

to the table.

The whole family eats breakfast together.

Oh, oh, Buffy wants his breakfast, too.

So Andy puts the dog food in his dish.

$D$addy has a big workbench in the garage. Right beside it is a little workbench that he made for Andy.

$\boxed{A}$ndy and Daddy like to work together. First Andy gets Daddy's hammer out of the tool drawer.

$\boxed{T}$hen he brings over the wood from the woodpile.

Daddy shows Andy how to use the hammer.

Then Andy uses his little hammer to hit the nail.

When they finish working, Andy puts away his tools.

Then they sweep the floor. Andy holds the dustpan for Daddy

and dumps the dirt into the trash can.

On some Saturdays Andy helps Daddy work on his car.

Daddy watches carefully while Andy uses his screwdriver.

$\boxed{A}$ndy sees Daddy checking the tire pressure.

$\boxed{A}$ndy also checks the pressure.

In the spring, Andy and Daddy have a lot of yard work to do.

They both put mulch in the wheelbarrow.

A ndy helps Daddy
push the big wheelbarrow.

T hey put the mulch
around their new tree, to
keep its roots moist.

Before he can fix the lawn mower, Daddy has to take the old gas out of it.

Andy works on his lawn mower, too.

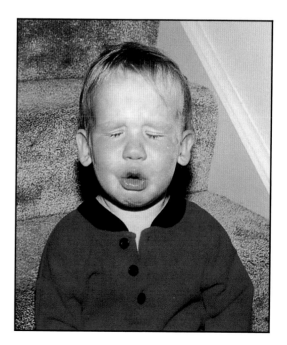

S|ometimes Andy does naughty things like climbing on the counter to reach the cookie jar

or tearing open Daddy's mail.

H|e is sad when Daddy makes him sit on the steps by himself.

$\boxed{A}$ndy and Steffie like to play hide-and-go-seek. Steffie shows Andy how to hide his eyes.

$\boxed{T}$hen Andy covers his eyes while Steffie hides.

He looks for Steffie behind the door.

But she is hiding under the chair.

Before bedtime Steffie and Andy play their drums.

Steffie has to cover her ears when Andy hits his upside-down pans.

After Mommy gives Andy his bath, he washes her face.

Mommy reads a story to Andy.

$\boxed{\text{T}}$hen Daddy carries Andy

to bed.

# AN AFTERWORD FOR PARENTS

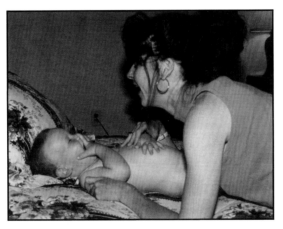

As they work together, Andy and his daddy are cultivating the all-important bond that is the foundation of their lifelong relationship. Since Andy's birth, bonding with both his parents has been fostered by good eye contact, smiles, frequent cuddling and prompt attention to his needs. Now that he is able to do things with Daddy, this bond becomes firmer with every project.

By inviting Andy to share in everyday activities, his daddy constantly models behavior patterns during the years when his son's urge to imitate is strongest. Andy wants to do almost everything that Daddy does. This points to the early years as an ideal opportunity to teach toddlers by example.

Like other two year-olds Andy can be impulsive, defiant and even have temper tantrums. But such behavior is minimized when he is engrossed in a project. As Andy senses the importance of being allowed to participate in family work, his conduct measures up to the trust that is placed in him. Andy has fun being helpful and eagerly learns good working habits.

Andy's daily activities provide a most natural and comfortable means for a two year-old to make the important transition from the so-called ''terrible twos'' — erratic behavior, such as throwing dog food on the floor, — to purposeful actions, such as pouring dog food carefully into the dog's dish.

As children focus on tasks that totally absorb their attention, they begin to show an observable improvement in behavior that is the basis for both later learning and character development.

This improvement usually comes about when they begin to use their hands purposefully rather than aimlessly. Maria Montessori, the world renowned educator, tells us that *"the hand is the chief teacher of the child"* . . . *"The child's intelligence,"* she wrote, *"can develop to a certain degree without the help of the hand. But if it develops with the hand, then the level it reaches is higher, and the child's character is stronger."*

When they use their hands for a specific purpose, children gradually lengthen their span of concentration. The importance of nourishing this ability during the early years of childhood cannot be overestimated. All later learning depends on concentration. Thus, the early focusing of attention begins a long-range preparation for formal education.

Andy's activities also reveal that he is gradually building confidence and a good self-image. How children feel about themselves affects nearly every aspect of their lives. Children form their first and strongest opinion about themselves in the family, and this initial impression is long-lasting. Therefore, negative experiences, even verbal put-downs, can be devastating; positive experiences and encouragement can be life-enhancing. To the extent that children feel they are lovable and capable, they build internal impressions of their essential goodness and ability to meet new challenges.

These internal impressions come from whatever happens to children in their everyday world. Their self-esteem is enhanced when they feel loved, when they participate in family fun, when they can do things for themselves and when they can perform essential tasks, no matter how small.

Parents nearly always want the best for their children; but the best is something that cannot be purchased. It can come only from themselves, when they give their children the gift of love and the gift of their time.

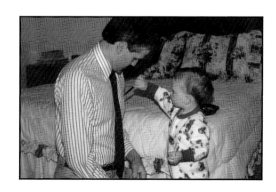

# A MESSAGE FROM ANDY'S DADDY

*I never had to encourage Andy to follow me around and do what I do. I cannot think of a time since he became mobile that he didn't insist on it. Given his age, I doubt if Andy has any particular outlook or opinion about what he should be doing; he has only his feelings. And I believe that nothing else would feel right to him.*

*As adults, we can look at things in a variety of ways. With the best intentions, we can envision handling Andy differently. We could confine him to cleaner, seemingly safer or more toy-oriented activities. We could limit the time he spends in my workshop and place him in more activities with children his own age. But we have learned there is no reason not to follow his lead and maintain the environment where he can do what comes most naturally to him.*

*Some might think this is giving Andy too much freedom around grown-up things. Actually, Andy is much better behaved when I allow him to explore the garage or garden while I do my work than when he is in the house, near the television or things he is told not to touch or climb on. His attention span is remarkably longer when he is using a small shovel or hammer, than when he is coloring or playing with toys. There were many days prior to Andy's second birthday that he worked two or three consecutive hours on the same project, especially with his small garden tools.*

*Obviously, there are limits and we must be vigilant. It takes time to set up an area where he can work safely, to stop and show him something, and to answer his endless list of questions. I like to think that he has never hurt himself handling some of my things because I am very cautious. But perhaps the reason is that while working with me he is not frustrated or defiant. He is exactly where he feels he should be.*

*After these experiences, the thought of preventing Andy from genuinely sharing in my everyday activities seems like something that would erode his enormous spirit. I am glad he was so insistent. Otherwise I may have missed out on this very rewarding part of my life. I encourage all parents to find or create such opportunities in their daily routines, so that this natural experience of bonding can take its wonderful course.*

Charles J. Wolf

# ABOUT PARENT CHILD PRESS

Parent Child Press, founded in 1975, is a unique publishing venture dedicated to enhancing early learning. Addressed to parents, teachers and other caregiving individuals, its publications stress the great importance of the environment during a child's earliest years and the far-reaching influence of the adult who is the most significant feature of a child's daily routine.

Many of the books, posters and slides published by Parent Child Press are the work of Aline D. Wolf whose experience as both a mother and teacher generates her many practical and creative suggestions.

The books and visual aids which she designs portray interesting learning ideas for children in environments ranging from kitchen to classroom. Essential to the success of these ideas are the adult attitudes which lead to productive interaction with children.

Each of Aline Wolf's publications, whether manual, fable, gift book or poster, is a unique creation springing from her desire to share a particular conviction with other adults who have responsibility for young children.

**Other books published by Parent Child Press**

*Look at the Child*
*A Book About Anna*
*The World of the Child*
*Peaceful Children, Peaceful World*
*Our Peaceful Classroom*
*Tutoring is Caring*
*Mommy, It's a Renoir!* — a manual for art appreciation for children.
Seven volumes of *Child-size Masterpieces* to be used with above manual.
*The Sense of Wonder Series* — six books for beginning readers.

Catalog available from Parent Child Press, PO Box 675, Hollidaysburg, PA 16648